★ SPORTS GREATS ★

TOP 10 HITTERS IN BASEBALL

David Aretha

Enslow Publishing
101 W. 23rd Street
Suite 240
New York, NY 10011
USA

enslow.com

Published in 2016 by Enslow Publishing, LLC
101 W. 23rd Street, Suite 240, New York, NY 10011

Library of Congress Cataloging-in-Publication Data
Aretha, David.
Top 10 hitters in Baseball / David Aretha.
pages cm. — (Sports greats)
Includes bibliographical references and index.
Summary: "Describes the ten greatest hitters in the history of baseball"— Provided by publisher.
Audience: Age: 8-up.
Audience: Grade: 4 to 6.
ISBN 978-0-7660-7396-8 (library binding)
ISBN 978-0-7660-7394-4 (pbk.)
ISBN 978-0-7660-7395-1 (6-pack)
1. Batting (Baseball)—United States—History—Juvenile literature. 2. Baseball players—Rating of—Juvenile literature. I. Title.
II. Title: Top ten hitters in baseball.
GV869.A74 2016
796.357'26—dc23
2015028584

Printed in the United States of America

To Our Readers: We have done our best to make sure all website addresses in this book were active and appropriate when we went to press. However, the author and the publisher have no control over and assume no liability for the material available on those websites or on any websites they may link to. Any comments or suggestions can be sent by e-mail to customerservice@enslow.com.

Photos Credits: Cover, p. 1 Jim McIsaac/Getty Images Sport/Getty Images; p. 4 Thearon W. Henderson/Getty Images Sports/Getty Images; pp. 5, 12 Transcendental Graphics/Getty Images Sports/Getty Images; pp. 7, 8 Mark Rucker/Transcendental Graphics, Getty Images Sports/Getty Images; p. 11 Louis Van Oeyen/Western Reserve Historical Society/Getty Images Sports/Getty Images; p. 15 Pictorial Parade/Archive Photos/Getty Images; p. 16 Hulton Archive/Archive Photos/Getty Images; pp. 19, 20 Frank Scherschel/The LIFE Picture Collection/Getty Images; p. 23 Rolls Press/Popperfoto/Getty Images; pp. 24, 27 Louis Requena/Major League Baseball/Getty Images; pp. 28, 32 Focus on Sport/Getty Images Sports/Getty Images; p. 31 Mitch Haddad/WireImage/Getty Images; p. 35 Tom Hauck /Allsport/Getty Images Sports/Getty Images; p. 36 TOSHIFUMI KITAMURA/AFP/Getty Images; p. 39 Sporting News via Getty Images; p. 40 Christian Petersen/Getty Images Sports/Getty Images; p. 43 Jared Wickerham/Getty Images North America/Getty Images; p. 44 Joel Auerbach/Getty Images Sports/Getty Images.

★ Contents ★

★ INTRODUCTION ★

Who is the greatest hitter ever? Ty Cobb? Babe Ruth? Nobody knows. While baseball geeks generate complex statistical formulas to compare hitters, they cannot determine if the Babe could outhit Miggy. The reason is that baseball was a lot different one hundred years ago, fifty years ago, and even twenty years ago than it is today.

In 1897, Wee Willie Keeler—all five-foot-four of him—batted .424 for the Baltimore Orioles. With one of the highest batting averages ever, Wee Willie mostly slapped singles past the infielders. "Hit 'em where they ain't" was his motto. Ty Cobb batted .366 in his career—tops in Major League Baseball (MLB) history. Babe Ruth was the first hitter to belt 30 home runs in a season—and the first to sock 40, 50, and 60. Prior to World War II, Cobb and Ruth were considered the best hitters of all time.

Albert Pujols started turning heads with his powerful hitting as soon as he reached the major leagues.

This century's hitters—such as Albert Pujols and Miguel Cabrera—may be the finest ever. That's because the pitchers they face today are far superior to those in the days of Ruth and Cobb. They are even better than during Tony Gwynn's heyday in the 1990s.

Forty years ago, few pitchers on a team threw 90 miles per hour (mph). Now, each club has several hurlers who fire at least 95 or even 100 mph. Aroldis Chapman once hit 106! Today's hitters have to face fresh relief specialists almost every game. In the ninth, the feared closer "slams the door" with searing gas and wicked benders.

Babe Ruth didn't let his taste for a good hot dog keep him from becoming one of baseball's top hitters.

Today's hitters are more physically fit than, say, Babe Ruth (who couldn't stop eating hot dogs). They also work with instructors from an early age and watch hitting videos to perfect their craft. Wee Willie didn't have those luxuries.

Could the Babe belt 40 homers in a season if he played today? Maybe—if he laid off the wieners and spent time in the film room. Could Pujols, without the advantages he has had, have blasted 40 longballs in the 1920s? We'll never know.

Get ready for the greatest hitters of baseball's various eras. They are a dream team of sluggers—a lineup for the ages.

★ Ty Cobb ★

Nickname:	*Georgia Peach*
Team:	*Detroit Tigers, 1905–1926; Philadelphia Athletics, 1927–1928*
Position:	*Outfield*
Number:	*None*
Year of Note:	*1911; batted .420 with 47 doubles, 24 triples, 83 stolen bases, 147 runs, and 127 RBI*

Ty Cobb was jealous of Babe Ruth. Throughout the early 1920s, everyone raved about the Babe and his mighty home runs. Cobb, they said, had the highest batting average of all time, but he was just a singles and doubles hitters.

Cobb preferred the style of baseball prevalent during his younger years: drilling line drives, beating out bunts, and stealing bases. But on May 5, 1925, he told a sportswriter, "I'll show you something today. I'm going for home runs for the first time in my career."

And sure enough, he did. Against the St. Louis Browns that afternoon, Cobb belted three home runs—plus a double and a couple singles. The next day, he walloped two more homers. Having proved his point, he went back to his style of play.

Unlike the jolly, friendly Ruth, Cobb was a nasty man who often got into fights. One day in New York, Cobb went into the stands and punched and kicked a heckler—a man who had lost eight fingers in machine accidents. "Cobb," someone cried, "that man has no hands!" "I don't care if he has no feet!" Ty replied while continuing to kick away.

Cobb focused some of his emotion into smacking the ball with all that he had.

Back in 1905, during Cobb's rookie season with the Detroit Tigers, a tragic accident fueled his anger. At their home in Georgia, Cobb's mother accidentally shot and killed his father. After that, Cobb played with "a fire in my belly," he once said. "Baseball was 100 percent of my life."

With fierce intensity and focus, Cobb slashed line drives all over the field. Other times, he beat out bunts and ground balls with his blazing speed. Once he reached first base, infielders rose to high alert. Cobb stole 897 bases in his career—a Major League Baseball record that would stand until 1977. The "Georgia Peach" looked for every edge he could. He kicked first base a couple inches away from the foul line so he could be a little closer to second base.

Ty Cobb said he played with a "fire in my belly." Maybe that's where he found the power to slug that ball.

He even sharpened the spikes on his cleats to intimidate middle infielders.

"The Babe was a great ballplayer, sure, but Cobb was even greater," said Hall of Famer Tris Speaker, when asked to compare the two. "Babe could knock your brains out, but Cobb would drive you crazy."

Cobb did most of his damage with his bat. From 1907 to 1919, he won the American League (AL) batting title twelve times. The man batted above .380 nine times, with highs of .401, .409, and even .420. His .366 career average is eight points higher than anyone else's. To this day, he ranks second all time in hits (4,191), runs scored (2,244), and triples (295).

Despite his prickly personality, Cobb was selected by 98.2 percent of the voters in the first Baseball Hall of Fame balloting. They just couldn't deny his extraordinary accomplishments. "I never saw anyone like Ty Cobb," said opposing player Casey Stengel. "No one even close to him. He was the greatest all-time ballplayer. That guy was superhuman."

★ BABE RUTH ★

Nickname:	*Sultan of Swat*
Teams:	*Boston Red Sox, 1914–1919; New York Yankees, 1920–1934; Boston Braves, 1935*
Position:	*Right field*
Number:	*3*
Year of Note:	*1927; belted .356 with 60 home runs and 165 RBI*

Kicked in the head by a horse, eleven-year-old Johnny Sylvester lay in a hospital bed in serious condition. That's when he received a note from his hero, Babe Ruth. "I'll knock a homer for you on Wednesday," it read. That Wednesday was Game 4 of the 1926 World Series, and Ruth blasted three home runs that afternoon for the New York Yankees. Reportedly inspired by his idol, Johnny dramatically improved.

A kid at heart, the Babe adored children. During Christmastime, he'd dress up as Santa Claus. After games, he'd sign autographs for long lines of boys and girls. But more than anything, Ruth loved to swing a bat. "I swing big, with everything I've got," he once said. Massive for his time at six-foot-two, 215 pounds, the Babe socked balls out of sight. In 1919, he set the Major League Baseball record for home runs in a season with 29. In 1920, he walloped 54—more than most American League teams hit that year.

Babe Ruth was always kind. He could even hit home runs for his fans!

George Herman "Babe" Ruth started out as a troublemaking kid in Baltimore—so much so that he was sent away to the St. Mary's Industrial School for Boys. There, Brother Matthias Boutlier taught him how to throw and hit. Ruth began his career as a tremendous pitcher for the Boston Red Sox, with a win–loss record of 89–46 from 1914 to 1919. Yet he was such a great hitter that the Yankees traded for him in 1920 and put him permanently in right field.

Ruth once said that if "I'd just tried for them dinky singles, I could've batted around .600." Instead, he swung for the seats—and the results were astounding. He led the American League in home runs twelve times, with highs of 54 (twice), 59 (1921), and 60 (1927). The Yankees broke attendance records as fans flocked to see their hitting hero. In Detroit, Ruth hit a ball clear out of Navin Field. It reportedly bounced off several cars and kept on going. Detroit News sportswriter Harry Salsinger claimed it traveled 885 feet before it stopped rolling.

"No one hit home runs the way Babe did," teammate Lefty Gomez once recalled. "They were something special…The ball

Not only could he knock the balls out of the park, but Ruth was a terrific pitcher, too.

would leave the bat, pause briefly, suddenly gain its bearings, then take off for the stands."

Because of his pitching and hitting ability, Ruth is universally regarded as the greatest player in baseball history. Many historians claim he is the number one hitter of all time. When he retired in 1935, he had crushed 714 home runs; the next guy on the list had hit just 353.

And it wasn't just home runs. Ruth batted .393 in 1923 and .342 for his career. His 2,214 runs batted in (RBI) rank second all time. He is third in walks with 2,062. He cracked so many hits and drew so many walks that he reached base safely 47.4 percent of the time. Ruth led the league in slugging percentage thirteen times, and his .690 slugging mark is the all-time record.

Someone once asked Ruth if he had any superstitions. "Just one," he replied. "Whenever I hit a home run, I make certain I touch all four bases."

★ Lou Gehrig ★

Nickname:	Iron Horse
Team:	New York Yankees, 1923–1939
Position:	First base
Number:	4
Year of Note:	1927; won AL MVP Award (.373 average, 47 homers, 173 RBI) and World Series

Lou Gehrig is one of sixteen Major League Baseball players to blast four home runs in a game. Incredibly, he almost made it five.

On June 3, 1932, in Philadelphia, his New York Yankees were in the midst of a 20–13 slugfest victory over the Athletics. Gehrig began his spree with three homers in the first five innings. In the seventh, he mashed one over the right field fence. In the ninth, fans watched in awe as the powerful first baseman drilled a shot to center field—the deepest part of the ballpark. Doc Cramer drifted all the way back to the wall to make the catch.

Weighing nearly fourteen pounds at birth—about double the size of the average baby—Lou seemed destined to hit home runs. While all three of his siblings died as children, Lou grew to become a tremendous athlete in New York City. As a seventeen-

Lou Gehrig played a record 2,130 games in a row. No one broke that record until Cal Ripken in 1995.

year-old in a high school game, he belted a ball completely out of Chicago's Wrigley Field. At Columbia University, he starred as a pitcher, first baseman, and football running back.

In a Columbia game, Yankees scout Paul Krichell watched as Gehrig "socked a couple of balls a mile. I sat up and took notice. I saw a tremendous youth, with powerful arms and terrific legs. I said, here is a kid who can't miss."

Gehrig became a full-time Yankees starter on June 2, 1925. First baseman Wally Pipp had a headache that day, so Gehrig replaced him—permanently. Beginning that day, the "Iron Horse" played 2,130 consecutive games, a record that would stand until Cal Ripken famously broke it in 1995.

For a decade, Babe Ruth and Gehrig formed the greatest slugging duo in history. While the headline-dominating Ruth belted a few more homers, the quiet Gehrig was nearly as good a hitter. From 1927 to 1937, Gehrig batted .350 while averaging 39 home runs and 154 RBI per season. Twice he led the league with 49 home runs, and his 185 RBI in 1931 remain an American

Not many players can boast eight World Series games with a batting average of .536, 7 home runs, and 17 RBI. But Lou Gehrig could.

League record. On six occasions, Gehrig helped lead the "Bronx Bombers" to the World Series title. In eight World Series games in 1928 and 1932—all Yankees victories—he batted .536 with 7 homers and 17 RBI!

Gehrig finished with a career average of .340, 493 home runs, and 1,995 RBI. He ranks third all-time in slugging percentage (.632) behind Babe Ruth and Ted Williams.

On May 2, 1939, Gehrig took his first day off in fourteen years. He was feeling weak and needed to see a doctor. It was soon discovered that he suffered from amyotrophic lateral sclerosis, an incurable muscular disease that results in death. From that point forward, it would be known as Lou Gehrig's disease.

Gehrig retired immediately at age thirty-five. On July 4, 1939, in front of teary-eyed fans at Yankee Stadium, he delivered a speech on Lou Gehrig Appreciation Day. He expressed his gratitude for all the wonderful people in his life. "I consider myself the luckiest man on the face of the Earth," he said. "And I might have been given a bad break, but I've got an awful lot to live for." Two years later, he was dead.

★ Ted Williams ★

Nickname: *Splendid Splinter*
Teams: *Boston Red Sox, 1939–1960*
Position: *Left field*
Number: *9*
Year of Note: *1941; batted .406 with 37 home runs and 120 RBI*

"All I want out of life," Ted Williams once said, "is that when I walk down the street folks will say, 'There goes the greatest hitter that ever lived.'"

Today, many baseball historians claim that the Boston Red Sox slugger was indeed the premier batsman of all time. Evidence abounds. For example, Williams remains the last Major League Baseball player to crack .400 in a season. Entering the final day of the 1941 campaign, he was batting .3996. That number rounded up to .400. Williams's manager, Joe Cronin, suggested that Williams take the day off so he could finish with that ".400" average. He refused, saying, "If I can't hit .400 all the way, I don't deserve it." Boston played a doubleheader that day, and Williams cracked six hits. He finished at .406.

Born and raised in San Diego, California, Williams spent his free time on the local ball fields. Tall and slender, he launched rainbow home runs and ripped line drives with a picture-perfect swing. He also had 20/10 vision. This meant that he could see from 20 feet what an average person sees at 10 feet. One ophthalmologist claimed that Ted's extraordinary vision was a "1 in 100,000 occurrence." He could see the spin of the seams on the baseball and determine if the pitch was a fastball or a curveball.

Ted Williams had amazing eyesight. He could see how the ball's seams were spinning during a pitch!

So Williams had the size (six-foot-three), swing, and vision to be a great hitter. He was also a fiercely determined man who studied the craft of hitting more than anyone. As a rookie in 1939, the "Splendid Splinter" batted .327 with 31 homers and 145 RBI. Twice he won the Triple Crown, meaning he led the league in batting average, home runs, and RBI. In 1949, he powered 43 homers and drove in 159 runs. In 1957, he batted .388.

Williams's .344 career average is the eighth best ever and the highest of any man born in the 1900s. Only Babe Ruth has a higher

Pitchers were afraid to throw strikes to the sharp-eyed Williams. He made it to base almost 50 percent of the time.

career slugging percentage than Williams's .634. "Teddy Ballgame" also walked a lot, due to his great eye at the plate and the fact that pitchers were afraid to throw him strikes. In all, he reached base safely 48.2 percent of the time—nearly half of his trips to the plate! No player in history has reached base at such a high rate.

Williams missed nearly five full seasons due to service in the military—first during World War II and then the Korean War. He finished with 521 home runs, and he probably would have belted another 150 or so had the world been a peaceful place.

At age forty-one in 1960, Williams rapped .316 but decided to retire. His last game fell on September 26, a dreary, frigid afternoon at Boston's Fenway Park. In the eighth inning, as he strode to the plate for his last-ever at bat, fans rose to their feet. On a 1-1 pitch, Ted blasted the ball deep to right-center field. It flew over the wall and crashed on the canopy above the Red Sox bullpen, 440 feet away.

Amid delirious applause, Williams rounded the bases and trotted coolly to the dugout—a fitting ending for the "greatest hitter that ever lived."

★ WILLIE MAYS ★

Nickname:	*Say Hey Kid*
Teams:	*New York Giants, 1951–1957; San Francisco Giants, 1958–1972; New York Mets, 1972–1973*
Position:	*Center field*
Number:	*24*
Year of Note:	*1954; socked 41 homers and won the batting title (.345), NL MVP Award, and World Series*

After going 0-for-5 on June 1, 1951, Willie Mays sat next to his locker and cried. As a rookie with the New York Giants, Mays was batting .038. He told his manager, Leo Durocher, that he couldn't hit major league pitching. Durocher replied, "As long as I'm the manager of the Giants, you are my center fielder...You are the best center fielder I've ever looked at."

After that little pep talk, Willie ripped .408 over the next thirteen games. A star was born.

Willie Mays was baseball's first "five-tool" player. He could hit for average, belt home runs, run, field, and throw at the highest of levels. Mays electrified the ballpark. His hat would often fly off his head as he sped around the bases. He dazzled in center field with his unique "basket" catches. His smile lit up the room. His penchant for saying "Say hey" upon greeting people earned him the nickname the "Say Hey Kid." Friendly to all, Mays often played stickball with kids on the streets of New York.

Mays was a champion hitter, but he succeeded at just about everything he did on the field. He was a super nice guy, too!

"If somebody came up and hit .450, stole 100 bases, and performed a miracle in the field every day, I'd still look you right in the eye and tell you that Willie was better," Durocher wrote in *Nice Guys Finish Last*. "He had the other magic ingredient that turns a superstar into a super Superstar. Charisma."

Mays grew up in Alabama during the Great Depression. He was so poor that he sometimes didn't wear shoes to school, but he had a positive attitude. He excelled in football and basketball in high school and later starred with the Birmingham Black Barons of baseball's Negro Leagues. In 1949, Giants scout Eddie Montague witnessed Mays's magic on the diamond. He reported to his boss, "You better send somebody down there with a barrelful of money and grab this kid."

Mays finished up his amazing career with a batting average of .302 and 660 homers! He was named an All-Star in twenty seasons.

In 1954, his first full major league season, Mays won the National League (NL) batting title (.345) and clubbed 41 home runs. In the World Series, he made the most famous catch in history. While sprinting toward the center field wall, he caught the ball over his shoulder—then turned and made a great throw to the infield. Mays led the NL in four-baggers in 1955 (51) and stolen bases the next four seasons. In one game for the San Francisco Giants in 1961, he walloped four home runs.

Mays was named to the MLB All-Star Game for twenty seasons in a row. As Ted Williams once said, "They invented the All-Star Game for Willie Mays." When Mays retired in 1973, he ranked third in Major League Baseball history in home runs (660) and second in runs scored (2,062). He was the first player ever with 300 stolen bases (338) and 300 homers. He is the only outfielder in history to make 7,000 catches.

To this day, many baseball experts claim that Mays was the greatest all-around player ever. No one admired him more than his old manager. "If he could cook," Durocher once quipped, "I'd marry him."

★ Hank Aaron ★

Nickname:	Hammerin' Hank
Teams:	Milwaukee Braves, 1954–1965; Atlanta Braves, 1966–1974; Milwaukee Brewers, 1975–1976
Position:	Right field
Number:	44
Year of Note:	1957; won NL MVP Award (44 homers) and World Series

Henry Aaron grew up poor and skinny in Mobile, Alabama, sometimes picking cotton to help his parents and seven siblings. His family couldn't afford baseball equipment, so Henry practiced hitting by swatting bottle caps with sticks. Some days, he'd upgrade to a broomstick.

Aaron's all African American high school didn't have a baseball team, so he played on a semiprofessional club team. Amazingly, he batted cross-handed. As a right-handed hitter, he held the bat with his left hand on top of his right. "Cross-handed means I was doing everything backwards," he told the Academy of Achievement. But "nobody ever taught me any different."

For Aaron, food was hard to come by, and at age fifteen he weighed only about 110 pounds. When he tried out with the

Brooklyn Dodgers that year (1949), "they just thought I was too small, and they just brushed me aside," he said in the Academy of Achievement interview.

Young Aaron held the bat with his left hand over his right. He later learned to bat correctly and became a legend at the plate.

Aaron began his career in the Negro Leagues, where he faced even more challenges. Because of their skin color, he and his teammates—the Indianapolis Clowns—were not allowed in many hotels and restaurants. After the players ate breakfast in a restaurant in Washington, D.C., the white workers smashed the dishes. In his autobiography titled *I Had a Hammer,* Aaron recalled that extremely humiliating experience: "Here we were in the capital in the land of freedom and equality, and they had to destroy the plates that had touched the forks that had been in the mouths of black men. If dogs had eaten off those plates, they'd have washed them."

Aaron learned to bat correctly and grew to become six-foot, 180 pounds. With powerful arms, he could hammer the ball, earning the nickname "Hammerin' Hank." He signed with the Boston

Aaron still holds the amazing all-time RBI record of 2,297! He never let anything get in the way of playing his best.

Braves in 1952 and debuted with the team in 1954 after it moved to Milwaukee.

In 1955, Aaron's legendary run of greatness began. He batted .314 with 27 home runs and made the NL All-Star team for the first of 21 consecutive seasons. In 1957, he walloped a league-high 44 homers and won the NL MVP Award. Then he bashed .393 with three homers in the 1957 World Series to defeat the mighty New York Yankees.

Quiet, kind, and highly respected, Aaron reached home run number 500 in 1968. He was thirty-four years old, and Babe Ruth's record of 714 four-baggers seemed far away. Yet Aaron's power didn't diminish during his late thirties, and he concluded the 1973 season with 713 home runs.

As he approached the record of the fabled Babe, Aaron received up to three thousand letters per day. Many were from fans, but some were racist and hateful. "You are [not] going to break this record established by the great Babe Ruth if I can help it," one person wrote. "My gun is watching your every black move."

Aaron found the threats stressful, but once more he overcame his challenges. On the night of April 8, 1974, on national television in Atlanta, Aaron belted a long flyball to left field. "That ball is gonna be... outta here!" blared Braves announcer Milo Hamilton. "It's gone! It's 715! There's a new home run champion of all-time, and it's Henry Aaron!"

Though Barry Bonds would break Aaron's record of 755 home runs in 2007, Hank Aaron still holds the all-time record for RBI: an incredible 2,297.

★ Tony Gwynn ★

Nickname:	*Mr. Padre*
Team:	*San Diego Padres, 1982–2001*
Position:	*Outfield*
Number:	*19*
Year of Note:	*1994; batted .394, the highest batting average in the major leagues since 1941*

Tony Gwynn loved people. Whether he was talking to players, reporters, or fans, he was always jolly, smiley, and laughing—pure joy to be around. But besides people, Gwynn had a special relationship with his bats.

"He loved his bats so much that for one year—1994, the year he almost hit .400—he told me he used basically one bat the entire year," baseball reporter Tim Kurkjian told WBUR radio. "And he told me the following spring training, taking batting practice on a back field alone with coach Rob Picciolo, he broke his bat. And he looked at me and he said, 'When I broke that bat, I almost started crying.'"

As a kid in Long Beach, California, Tony and his brother were obsessed with the game. When they weren't belting a baseball, they were "hitting a fig or hitting a sock ball or hitting a wad of tape," he said in his Hall of Fame acceptance speech.

A tremendous athlete, Gwynn starred in baseball and basketball at the University of San Diego. He claimed that his many years of dribbling strengthened his wrists, which improved his hitting. In 1981, both the San Diego Padres and the San Diego Clippers (of the National Basketball Association, or NBA) drafted him, and he chose baseball.

In 1981, the talented Tony Gwynn was drafted by the San Diego Padres and the NBA's San Diego Clippers.

As a third-round pick, Gwynn wasn't a lock to reach the major leagues. Most of the other third-round selections that year never reached the majors. Scout Gordon Lakey wrote about him: "Very good fastball hitter with excellent bat speed…Could be a good hitter some day.

Lakey didn't realize two things about Tony Gwynn: The man had extraordinary eyesight as well as a tremendous desire to

Gwynn could see the details of a pitch. He also watched videos of his hitting to look for and correct mistakes.

improve his hitting. Regarding his eyes, pitcher Greg Maddux told *Washington Post* writer Thomas Boswell, "If a pitcher can change speeds, every hitter is helpless, limited by human vision—except for that [bleeping] Tony Gwynn."

Gwynn ripped .347 in 175 minor league games, but he was hitting only .229 with the Padres on July 29, 1983. That's when he started analyzing videotape of all his swings. This became his career-long obsession. He constantly examined his flaws and then perfected his swing in the batting cages.

Beginning in 1983, Gwynn hit above .300 for nineteen years in a row. He won eight NL batting crowns, with highs of .370 (1987), .394 (1994), and .372 (1997). In addition, he was an award-winning defensive outfielder and a terrific base stealer. "Mr. Padre" finished his career with 3,141 hits and 319 stolen bases. His career average of .338 is the highest of any player born after World War I.

After his Hall of Fame career, Gwynn coached at San Diego State for twelve seasons. Tragically, his addiction to chewing tobacco resulted in cancer of a salivary gland. He died on June 16, 2014, at age fifty-four. "Major League Baseball today mourns the tragic loss of Tony Gwynn," said MLB commissioner Bud Selig, "the greatest Padre ever and one of the most accomplished hitters that our game has ever known."

★ Ichiro Suzuki ★

Nickname:	Wizard
Teams:	Seattle Mariners, 2001–2012; New York Yankees, 2012–2014; Miami Marlins, 2015
Position:	Right field
Number:	51
Year of Note:	2004; ripped .372 with MLB-record 262 hits

On a beautiful night in Seattle, Ichiro Suzuki held his bat high with his right hand. It's what he does before every pitch, but this time he was about to wield magic. Against the Texas Rangers, Suzuki swung and ripped a single up the middle. The packed crowd went wild. Fireworks exploded. Teammates rushed out of the dugout. And on the scoreboard, the "Ichiro Hit Count" jumped from 257 to 258. He had just broken George Sisler's major league record for most hits in a season.

As dramatic music rocked Safeco Field, Seattle players hugged their beloved teammate. "I think that's the most emotional I've ever gotten in my life," Suzuki said after the game.

"You can tell how happy and proud I am just by looking at me," his father, Nobuyuki, told a reporter in Japan. "The tears just won't stop flowing."

Back in the early 1980s, Nobuyuki taught his son how to play baseball in the town of Toyoyama, Japan. Each day, little Ichiro would hit 250 pitches from a machine and 250 from his father. In a country that took "America's game" very seriously, Ichiro stood out on the diamond. The slender boy built strength by throwing car tires and hitting Wiffle balls with a heavy shovel.

As a tiny player, Ichiro Suzuki knew he needed to build up strength. He threw car tires and used a heavy shovel as a bat.

At age eighteen in 1992, Suzuki debuted in the Pacific League—Japan's equivalent of the major leagues. He didn't play much because his manager didn't like how he hit. Suzuki shifted his weight forward during the swing (considered a no-no) and slapped at the ball. For Suzuki, it worked. In 1994, he ripped .385 to win his first of seven consecutive Pacific League batting titles. A year later, he stole 49 bases while swatting 25 home runs.

Before setting a ML record with ten straight 200-hit seasons, Ichiro Suzuki was a seven-time batting champion in Japan.

In 2001, Suzuki made history by becoming the first Japanese-born non-pitcher to play in the major leagues. Immediately, Americans marveled at the player who simply went by one name: Ichiro. As a rookie for Seattle, he led the American League in batting (.350) and hits (242). In right field, he won his first of ten straight Gold Glove Awards. He stunned base runners with his long, blazing throws. In one game, as he flew to first base on a ground ball, New York Yankees star Derek Jeter exclaimed, "Wow!" He excited his countrymen so much that many fans flew halfway around the world to watch him play for the Mariners. At the end of his rookie year, he was named the American League MVP.

From 2001 to 2010, Suzuki averaged .331 with 38 steals per year. He also reached 200 hits for ten consecutive seasons—a Major League Baseball record. How did he do it? Practice. Concentration. Amazing vision. Lightning-quick reflexes. "The way he hits is just like a Samurai," said Japanese fan Isao Ogata. "I'll bet he could split a mosquito with a sword."

For the Yankees on August 21, 2013, Ichiro stroked his 4,000th career hit—Pacific League and major leagues combined. Once again, teammates swarmed the field to congratulate him. "It's an amazing feat," Yankees manager Joe Girardi told the press. "It's a testament to how hard he's worked, how long he's been in the game, how he stays healthy, the way he goes about his business. He's a great player, and he's been a great player for a long time."

★ Albert Pujols ★

Nickname:	*Prince Albert*
Teams:	*St. Louis Cardinals, 2001–2011; Los Angeles Angels of Anaheim, 2012–present*
Position:	*First base*
Number:	*5*
Year of Note:	*2006; bashed .331 with 49 homers and 137 RBI and won World Series title*

In the ninth inning of Game 3 of the 2011 World Series, Albert Pujols blasted his third home run of the game. But as he returned to the dugout after his home run trot, Pujols was surprised by the greeting. His St. Louis Cardinals teammates were not congratulating him. They sat on the bench, stone-faced, acting like he had just grounded out.

Pujols must have wondered what was the matter. Were they mad at him? Jealous, perhaps, of all his success? Nah! They were just pulling a prank! After a few seconds, the players jumped to their feet, grinned, and hugged the hitting hero. After all, if it weren't for Pujols, they wouldn't have won the 2011 World

In 2001, Albert Pujols had an amazing rookie season. His batting average was .329. He also hit 37 homers and had a 130 RBI.

Series title. "He's a guy who can carry you all the way through the playoffs," teammate Skip Schumaker told the press. "And we're not afraid to hop on his back and ride on."

The legend of Albert Pujols began in Santo Domingo, Dominican Republic. Poor as a child, he played catch with limes and a cut-off milk carton. When he was a teenager, his family moved to New York City and then Independence, Missouri. That's where he wowed his Osage High School baseball coach, Dave Fry. "Here's this big, strong, good-looking kid just standing there smiling, saying he wants to play *beisbol*," Fry told a *Los Angeles Times* reporter. "It was like a gift from the baseball gods."

Albert spent just one year (2000) in the minor leagues. In 2001, he had perhaps the greatest rookie season ever, belting .329 with 37 homers and 130 RBI. Opponents soon realized that the kid had no weaknesses in his swing. "Left-hander, right-hander, soft thrower, power guy, fastballs away, fastballs in—he doesn't have any holes," Cardinals teammate Tino Martinez once said. He was also so dang strong that his line drives sailed over the fence. Mike

In 2015, Pujols was hitting as strong as ever. He started the season with a whopping 520 homers.

Trout, the 2014 AL MVP, idolized Pujols as a kid. "Every time you turned on Xbox or PlayStation, you always wanted to pick Albert," Trout told the *Los Angeles Times*.

In each of his first ten seasons, Pujols batted more than .300 while exceeding 30 home runs and 100 RBI. He also won the NL MVP Award three times: in 2005, 2008, and 2009.

Recently, a debate has raged: Who's the greatest hitter of the twenty-first century? There are only two candidates: Pujols and Miguel Cabrera. While Cabrera hit .320 with 390 homers and 1,369 RBI over his first twelve seasons, Pujols ripped .325-475-1,434. So statistically, Pujols wins. And if he's the best hitter of the twenty-first century, he may be the greatest batsman of all time. After all, the pitching today is far superior to that of the 1900s.

In 2015, Pujols was still going strong at age thirty-five. He entered the season with 520 home runs, and he served as a mentor to such players as Trout, his Los Angeles Angels teammate. "It's pretty wild to be in the same clubhouse with him, to see him chase history," Trout said. "I pick his brain every chance I get."

★ Miguel Cabrera ★

Nickname:	Miggy
Teams:	Florida Marlins, 2003–2007; Detroit Tigers, 2008–present
Positions:	First base; third base
Number:	24
Year of Note:	2012; won AL Triple Crown with .330 average, 44 homers, and 139 RBI

On a warm August night in New York in 2013, the Detroit Tigers' 12-game winning streak was about to end. Or so it seemed. With two outs in the ninth inning, the Yankees led 3–1. Detroit had a man on second base, but Mariano Rivera—the greatest relief pitcher ever—stood on the mound. He was winning the battle against Miguel Cabrera, the best hitter of the twenty-first century after Albert Pujols.

On a 1-2 pitch, "Miggy" fouled the ball off his knee. He limped around in pain for more than a minute before bravely returning to the batter's box. "He only needs one leg anyway," said Tigers broadcaster Mario Impemba. On the next pitch, Cabrera fouled the ball off his foot. Again he limped in pain . . . until breaking into a smile. Cabrera waddled back to the box, took a ball outside, and then...

"High flyball, center field!" blared Impemba. "[Brett] Gardner going back—still going back! Track! Wall! And gone! Un... believable!"

Rivera looked stunned while a group of Tigers fans danced in the stands. Although Detroit lost the game, the Tigers won their third straight American League Central Division title in 2013. They could thank Cabrera, who captured his second consecutive AL Most Valuable Player Award. As retired pitcher Ed Farmer said during a Chicago White Sox broadcast, Cabrera "might be the greatest hitter ever."

Cabrera grew up in Venezuela, where his mother played shortstop for the country's national softball team. His dad was a terrific baseball player, and so was young Miguel, who began playing in national competitions at age six. He signed a professional contract at age sixteen, and four years later he blasted a home run in the 2003 World Series for the Florida Marlins.

Miguel Cabrera has the size and the muscles to really slug the ball, no matter what kind of pitch comes at him.

The friendly, joking Cabrera gets serious in the batter's box. Thanks to that focus, in 2014 he walloped an eleventh straight season of more than 100 RBIs.

A big, muscular basher, Cabrera could hit any pitch in the strike zone. In his four full seasons with the Marlins, he hit a combined .318 and averaged 32 home runs per year. Traded to Detroit in 2008, he got even better. Chicago White Sox announcer Hawk Harrelson called him the smartest hitter of his generation. Miggy won the AL batting title in 2011 (.344), and a year later he became the first player since 1967 to win a Triple Crown. That meant he led the league in batting (.330), homers (44), and RBI (139).

The next season, 2013, he was just as spectacular. "I'm seeing things that are a little mind-boggling," Tigers manager Jim Leyland told the press. Cabrera won the 2013 batting crown (.348) while tallying 44 homers and 137 RBI. In 2014, he topped 100 RBI for the eleventh straight season. If he can stay healthy over the next decade, he has a shot at breaking Hank Aaron's major league record for career RBI.

Besides his heroic hitting, Cabrera has a childlike enthusiasm for the game. He is always smiling, and while playing first base he jokes and chitchats with opposing base runners. Only in the batter's box does Cabrera get serious. In a series at Cleveland in 2015, Miggy crushed 11 hits in 14 at bats. The Indians eventually gave up. In his final at bat of the series, they intentionally walked him—even though there was already a runner on first base.

★ GLOSSARY ★

batsman—Another name for a hitter.

batting average—A statistic: hits divided by official at bats (walks, hit-by-pitches, sacrifice flies, and sacrifice bunts don't count as official at bats).

batting title/batting crown—The highest batting average in the league, be it the American League, National League, or some other league.

change-up—A pitch that's thrown with the same arm motion as a fastball but isn't as fast; the speed change is meant to fool the hitter.

closer—A team's relief pitcher who typically pitches in the ninth inning to preserve the team's lead.

doubleheader—When two teams play two games against each other in one day.

four-bagger—Another term for a home run.

Gold Glove Award—An award bestowed annually by Rawlings to the best defensive player at each position in each league, American and National.

longball—Another name for a home run.

middle infielder—A player who plays second base or shortstop.

Most Valuable Player (MVP)—A sports award presented to a team or league's best player.

Negro Leagues—Professional leagues for African Americans; played during an era when African Americans were not allowed to play in the major leagues.

repertoire—A pitcher's assortment of pitches; one pitcher's repertoire may include a fastball, curveball, and change-up.

runs batted in (RBI)—The number of base runners a batter drives in, either with a base hit, walk, hit-by-pitch, flyout, or groundout.

set-up reliever—A relief pitcher who typically pitches in the seventh or eighth inning.

slugger—A good hitter with home run power.

slugging percentage—A statistic: total bases divided by official at bats; total bases are defined as one base for a single, two bases for a double, three bases for a triple, and four bases for a home run.

stickball—A game played on city streets using a stick and a ball; similar to baseball.

★ FURTHER READING ★

Books

Graves, Will. *The Best MLB Hitters of All Time*. Edina, MN: ABDO Publishing, 2014.

Stout, Glenn. *Baseball Heroes*. Boston, MA: Houghton Mifflin, 2011.

Williams, Doug. *Hank Aaron: Groundbreaking Baseball Slugger*. Edina, MN: ABDO Publishing, 2014.

Winter, Jonah. *You Never Heard of Willie Mays?!* New York, NY: Random House, 2013.

Young, Jeff C. *Albert Pujols: A Baseball Star Who Cares*. New York, NY: Enslow Publishers, 2014.

Websites

Baseball-Reference.com

www.baseball-reference.com

Includes endless statistics on every player in Major League Baseball history.

MLB.com/Kids

mlb.mlb.com/mlb/kids

Leads you to the kid sites of all thirty Major League Baseball teams.

National Baseball Hall of Fame

baseballhall.org

Includes profiles on every member of the Hall of Fame, including videos of many.

★ INDEX ★